Merry Christmas,
Mary!

Love, Aunt Kate

# THE
# CAT LOVER'S
## QUOTATION BOOK

# THE
# CAT LOVER'S
## QUOTATION BOOK

### A Collection of
### Feline Favorites

Hatherleigh Press is committed to preserving and protecting the natural resources of the earth. Environmentally responsible and sustainable practices are embraced within the company's mission statement.

Visit us at www.hatherleighpress.com and register online for free offers, discounts, special events, and more.

*The Cat Lover's Quotation Book*

Text Copyright © 2016 Hatherleigh Press

Library of Congress Cataloging-in-Publication Data is available.
ISBN: 978-1-57826-623-4

Printed in the United States
10 9 8 7 6 5 4 3 2

# CONTENTS

WHEN GOD made the world, He chose to put animals in it, and decided to give each whatever it wanted. All the animals formed a long line before His throne, and the cat quietly went to the end of the line. To the elephant and the bear He gave strength, to the rabbit and the deer, swiftness; to the owl, the ability to see at night, to the birds and the butterflies, great beauty; to the fox, cunning; to the monkey, intelligence; to the dog, loyalty; to the lion, courage; to the otter, playfulness. And all these were things the animals begged of God. At last he came to the end of the line, and there sat the little cat, waiting patiently. "What will you have?" God asked the cat.

The cat shrugged modestly. "Oh, whatever scraps you have left over. I don't mind."

"But I'm God. I have everything left over."

"Then I'll have a little of everything, please."

And God gave a great shout of laughter at the cleverness of this small animal, and gave the cat everything she asked for, adding grace and elegance and, only for her, a gentle purr that would always attract humans and assure her a warm and comfortable home.

But he took away her false modesty.

— LENORE FLEISCHER,
  "When God Made Cats"

# DIVINE
# FELINES

He seems the incarnation of everything soft and silky and velvety, without a sharp edge in his composition, a dreamer whose philosophy is sleep and let sleep.

SAKI

Thousands of years ago, cats were worshiped as gods. Cats have never forgotten this.

AUTHOR UNKNOWN

In the beginning, God created man, but seeing him so feeble, He gave him the cat.

WARREN ECKSTEIN

Poets generally love cats—because poets have no delusions about their own superiority.

MARION GARRETTY

The really great thing about cats is their endless variety. One can pick a cat to fit almost any kind of decor, income, personality, mood. But under the fur, there still lies, essentially unchanged, one of the world's free souls.

ERIC GURNEY

Sometimes he will sit on the carpet in front of you, looking at you with eyes so melting, so caressing and so human, that they almost frighten you, for it is impossible to believe that a soul is not there.

THEOPHILE GAUTIER

If man could be crossed with the cat, it would improve man, but deteriorate the cat.

MARK TWAIN

A cat pours his body on the floor like water. It is restful just to see him.

WILLIAM LYON PHELPS

I believe cats to be spirits come to earth.
A cat, I am sure, could walk on a cloud
without coming through.

JULES VERNE

If you are worthy of its affection, a cat will
be your friend but never your slave.

THEOPHILE GAUTIER

If a fish is the movement of water embod-
ied, given shape, then a cat is a diagram
and pattern of subtle air.

DORIS LESSING

I put down my book, *The Meaning of Zen*, and see the cat smiling into her fur as she delicately combs it with her rough pink tongue. "Cat, I would lend you this book to study but it appears you have already read it."

She looks up and gives me her full gaze. "Don't be ridiculous," she purrs, "I wrote it."

Dilys Laing

If there were to be a universal sound depicting peace, I would surely vote for the purr.

Barbara L. Diamond

The reason cats climb is so that they can look down on almost every other animal— it's also the reason they hate birds.

K.C. BUFFINGTON

Her ears, lightly fringed with white that looked silver, lifted and moved, back, forward, listening and sensing. Her face turned, slightly, after each new sensation, alert. Her tail moved, in another dimension, as if its tip was catching messages her other organs could not. She sat poised, air-light, looking, hearing, feeling, smelling, breathing, with all of her, fur, whiskers, ears—everything, in delicate vibration.

DORIS LESSING

The dog may be wonderful prose, but only the cat is poetry.

FRENCH PROVERB

Cats were put into the world to disprove the dogma that all things were created to serve man.

PAUL GRAY

Human beings are drawn to cats because they are all we are not—self-contained, elegant in everything they do, relaxed, assured, glad of company, yet still possessing secret lives.

PAM BROWN

I have lived with several Zen masters—all of them cats.

ECKHART TOLLE

The cat has been described as the most perfect animal, the acme of muscular perfection and the supreme example in the animal kingdom of the coordination of mind and muscle.

R. AMBROSE-BROWN

The way to get on with a cat is to treat it as an equal—or even better, as the superior it knows itself to be.

ELIZABETH PETERS

Cats, no less liquid than their shadows, offer no angles to the wind. They slip, diminished, neat, through loopholes less than themselves.

A.S.J. TESSIMOND

A little lion, small and dainty sweet with sea-grey eyes and softly stepping feet.

GRAHAM TOMSON

Like a graceful vase, a cat, even when motionless, seems to flow.

GEORGE F. WILL

A cat's rage is beautiful, burning with pure cat flame, all its hair standing up and crackling blue sparks, eyes blazing and sputtering.

WILLIAM S. BURROUGHS

Her conscious tail her joy declared...
The velvet of her paws,
Her coat, that with the tortoise
     views,
Her ears of jet and emerald eyes,
She saw, and purr'd applause.

THOMAS GRAY

With the qualities of cleanliness, affection, patience, dignity, and courage that cats have, how many of us, I ask you, would be capable of becoming cats?

FERNAND MERY

And let me touch those curving claws of yellow ivory; and grasp the tail that like a monstrous asp coils round your heavy velvet paws.

OSCAR WILDE

The cat is the animal to whom the creator gave the biggest eyes, the softest fur, the most supremely delicate nostrils, a mobile ear, an unrivaled paw and a curved claw borrowed from the rose tree.

SIDONIE-GABRIELLE COLETTE

As every cat owner knows, nobody owns a cat.

ELLEN PERRY BERKELEY

I have studied many philosophers and many cats. The wisdom of cats is infinitely superior.

HIPPOLYTE TAINE

A cat isn't fussy—just so long as you remember he likes his milk in the shallow, rose-patterned saucer and his fish on the blue plate. From which he will take it, and eat it off the floor.

ARTHUR BRIDGES

Dogs believe they are human. Cats believe they are God.

AUTHOR UNKNOWN

If cleanliness is next to godliness, surely our cats must go to heaven and sit on the arm of God's throne.

JERRY CLIMER

In the middle of a world that has always been a little bit mad, a cat walks with confidence.

ROSEANNE AMBERSON

I love cats. I love their grace and their elegance. I love their independence and their arrogance, and the way they lie and look at you, summing you up, surely to your detriment, with that unnerving, unwinking, appraising stare.

JOYCE STRANGER

Cats have it all—admiration, an endless sleep, and company only when they want it.

ROD MCKUEN

The cat is the only animal which accepts the comforts but rejects the bondage of domesticity.

GEORGES LOUIS LECLERC
DE BUFFON

# MISCHIEF
# AND
# MYSTERY

Prowling his own quiet backyard or asleep
by the fire, he is still only a whisker away
from the wilds.

JEAN BURDEN

Always the cat remains a little beyond the
limits we try to set for him in our blind
folly.

ANDRE NORTON

Nature breaks through the eyes of the cat.

IRISH PROVERB

Among human beings, a cat is merely a cat; among cats, a cat is a prowling shadow in the jungle.

KAREL CAPEK

A cat is a puzzle for which there is no solution.

HAZEL NICHOLSON

After dark all cats are leopards.

ZUNI NATIVE AMERICAN
PROVERB

It always gives me a shiver when I see a cat seeing what I can't see.

ELEANOR FARJEON

If cats could talk, they wouldn't.

NAN PORTER

The cat has nine lives—three for playing, three for straying, and three for staying.

ENGLISH PROVERB

When she walked...she stretched out long and thin like a little tiger, and held her head high to look over the grass as if she were treading the jungle.

SARAH ORNE

To assume a cat's asleep is a grave mistake. He can close his eyes and keep both his ears awake.

AILEEN FISHER

In nine lifetimes, you'll never know as much about your cat as your cat knows about you.

MICHEL DE MONTAIGNE

The cat, which is a solitary beast, is single minded and goes its way alone, but, the dog, like his master, is confused in his mind.

H.G. WELLS

The cat of the slums and alleys, starved, outcast, harried... still displays the self-reliant watchfulness which man has never taught it to lay aside.

SAKI

Way down deep, we're all motivated by the same urges. Cats have the courage to live by them.

JIM DAVIS

Every dog has his day—but the nights are reserved for the cats.

AUTHOR UNKNOWN

Cats are absolute individuals, with their own ideas about everything, including the people they own.

JOHN DINGMAN

When my cats aren't happy, I'm not happy. Not because I care about their mood but because I know they're just sitting there thinking up ways to get even.

PENNY WARD MOSER

He lives in the half lights, in secret places, free and alone—this little great being whom his mistress call, "My Cat."

MARGARET BENSON

The cat has a nervous ear,
that turns this way and that.
And what the cat may hear,
is known but to the cat.

DAVID MORTON

# PURRFECT
# PERSONALITY

There are three basic personality factors in cats: The kind who run up when you say hello and rub against you in cheap romance; the kind who run away certain that you mean to ravish them; and the kind who just look back and don't move a muscle. I love all three kinds.

EVE BABITZ

One reason we admire cats is for their proficiency in one-upmanship. They always seem to come out on top, no matter what they are doing, or pretend they do.

BARBARA WEBSTER

If you, Like me
Were made of fur
And sun warmed you,
Like me You'd purr,

KARLA KUSKIN

Dogs...can be made to feel guilty about anything, including the sins of their owners. Cats refuse to take the blame for anything—including their own sins.

ELIZABETH PETERS

Cats seem to go on the principle that it never does any harm to ask for what you want.

JOSEPH WOOD KRUTCH

My cat speaks sign language with her tail.

ROBERT A. STERN

Cats speak a subtle language in which few sounds carry many meanings, depending on how they are sung or purred. "Mnrhnh" means comfortable soft chairs. It also means fish. It means genial companionship...and the absence of dogs.

VAL SCHAFFNER

In my house lives a cat who is a curmudgeon and cantankerous, a cat who is charming and convivial, and a cat who is combative and commendable. And yet I have but one cat.

DAVE EDWARD

Cats' hearing apparatus is built to allow the human voice to easily go in one ear and out the other.

STEPHEN BAKER

Cats, as you know, are quite impervious to threats.

CONNIE WILLIS

Cats choose us; we don't own them.

KRISTIN CAST

Cats invented self-esteem. There is not an insecure bone in their body.

ERMA BOMBECK

A cat has absolute emotional honesty; human beings, for one reason or another, may hide their feelings but a cat does not.

ERNEST HEMINGWAY

Cats know how to obtain food without labor, shelter without confinement and love without penalties.

W.L. GEORGE

A cat sees no good reason why it should obey another animal, even if it does stand on two legs.

SARAH THOMPSON

Guilt isn't in cat vocabulary. They never suffer remorse for eating too much, sleeping too long or hogging the warmest cushion in the house. They welcome every pleasurable moment as it unravels and savor it to the full until a butterfly or falling leaf diverts their attention. They don't waste energy counting the number of calories they've consumed or the hours they've frittered away sunbathing.

Helen Brown

Anyone who claims that a cat cannot give a dirty look has either never kept a cat or is singularly unobservant.

Maurice Burton

Cats always know whether people like or dislike them. They do not always care enough to do anything about it.

WINIFRED CARRIERE

The great charm of cats is their rampant egotism, their devil-may-care attitude toward responsibility, their disinclination to earn an honest dollar.

ROBERTSON DAVIES

Cats must have three names—an everyday name such as Peter; a more particular, dignified name such a Quaxo, Bombalurina, or Jellylorum; and thirdly, the name the cat thinks up for himself, his deep and inscrutable singular Name.

T.S. ELIOT

When I returned home at night, he was pretty sure to be waiting for me near the gate and would rise and saunter along the walk, as though his being there was purely accidental.

CHARLES DUDLEY WARNER

When I meow it means...I am hungry...I want food in my bowl...I want food in my bowl right now...I want to go out...I want to come in...Brush me...Get my toy out from under the sofa...It's time to change the litter...I just put a mouse in the bureau drawer...I did not break that vase...Get me down from this tree...Please kill that dog next door...Hello...Goodbye.

HENRY BEARD

Cats hate a closed door, you know, regardless of which side they're on. If they're out, they want to get in, and if they're in, they want to get out.

LILIAN JACKSON BRAUN

If I called her she would pretend not to hear, but would come a few moments later when it could appear that she had thought of doing so first.

ARTHUR WEIGALL

Cats randomly refuse to follow orders to prove they can.

ILONA ANDREWS

Who among us hasn't envied a cat's ability to ignore the cares of daily life and to relax completely?

Karen Brademeyer

There is nothing in the animal world, to my mind, more delightful than grown cats at play. They are so swift and light and graceful, so subtle and designing, and yet so richly comic.

Monica Edwards

The animal has more liberty than the cat... the cat is the best anarchist.

Ernest Hemingway

If animal could speak, the dog would be a blundering outspoken fellow; but the cat would have the rare grace of never saying a word too much.

MARK TWAIN

The cat has too much spirit to have no heart.

ERNEST MENAUL

Most of us rather like our cats to have a streak of wickedness. I should not feel quite easy in the company of any cat that walked about the house with a saintly expression.

BEVERLY NICHOLS

Few animals display their mood via facial expressions as distinctly as cats.

KONRAD LORENZ

With a cat, you stand on much the same footing as you stand with a fine and dignified friend; if you forfeit his respect, the relationship suffers. The cat, it is well to remember, remains the friend of Man because it pleases him to do so, not because he must.

CARL VAN VECHTEN

A cat is there when you call her—if she doesn't have something better to do.

BILL ADLER

Cats are cats...the world over! These intelligent, peace-loving, four-footed friends—who are without prejudice, without hate, without greed—may someday teach us something.

LILLIAN JACKSON BRAUN

Women and cats will do as they please, and men and dogs should relax and get used to the idea.

ROBERT A. HEINLEIN

I would like to see anyone, prophet, king or God, convince a thousand cats to do the same thing at the same time.

NEIL GAIMAN

Cats have a scam going—you buy the food, they eat the food, they go away; that's the deal.

EDDIE IZZARD

If a dog jumps in your lap, it is because he is fond of you; but if a cat does the same thing, it is because your lap is warmer.

ALFRED NORTH WHITEHEAD

The mathematical probability of a common cat doing exactly as it pleases is the one scientific absolute in the world.

LYNN M. OSBAND

I don't think it is so much the actual bath that most cats dislike; I think it's the fact that they have to spend a good part of the day putting their hair back in place.

DEBBIE PETERSON

Meow is like "aloha"—it can mean anything.

HANK KETCHUM

There are people who reshape the world by force or argument, but the cat just lies there, dozing, and the world quietly reshapes itself to suit his comfort and convenience.

ALLEN & IVY DODD, "A Tale of Two Cats"

Acrobat, diplomat,
and simple tabby-cat,
He conjures tangled forests
in a furnished flat.

MICHAEL HAMBURGER

Dogs come when they're called. Cats take a
message and get back to you later.

MARY BLY

You now have learned enough to see
That Cats are much like you and me
And other people whom we find
Possessed of various types of mind.
For some are sane and some are mad
And some are good and some are bad

And some are better, some are worse—
But all may be described in verse.

> T.S. ELIOT,
>> "The Ad-dressing of Cats,"

Cats are rather delicate creatures and they are subject to a good many ailments, but I never heard of one who suffered from insomnia.

> JOSEPH WOOD KRUTCH.

# KITTENS

They say the test of literary power is whether a man can write an inscription. I say, can he name a kitten?

SAMUEL BUTLER

A kitten is in the animal world what a rosebud is in the garden.

ROBERT SOUTHEY

A kitten is the delight of a household. All day long, comedy is played by an incomparable actor.

CHAMPFLEURY

When you invite a kitten into your home, you bring indoors something slightly wild, often unpredictable and always entertaining.

BARBARA L. DIAMOND

Listen, Kitten, get this clear;
This is my chair, I sit here.
Okay, Kitty, we can share;
When I'm not home, it's your
    chair...

RICHARD SHAW

Four little Persians, but one only looked in my direction. I extended a tentative finger and two soft paws clung to it. There was a contented sound of purring, I suspect on both our parts.

GEORGE FREEDLEY

Kittens are born with their eyes shut. They open them in about six days, take a look around, then close them again for the better part of their lives.

STEPHEN BAKER

A kitten is so flexible that she is almost double; the hind parts are equivalent to another kitten with which the forepart plays. She does not discover that her tail belongs to her until you tread on it.

HENRY DAVID THOREAU

A kitten is the most irresistible comedian in the world. Its wide-open eyes gleam with wonder and mirth. It darts madly at nothing at all, and then, as though suddenly checked in the pursuit, prances sideways on its hind legs with ridiculous agility and zeal.

AGNES REPPLIER

Who would believe such pleasure from a wee ball o' fur?

IRISH SAYING

What marvelous vitality a kitten has. It is really something very beautiful the way life bubbles over in the little creatures. They rush about, and mew, and spring; dance on their hind legs, embrace everything with their front ones, roll over and over, lie on their backs and kick. They don't know what to do with themselves, they are so full of life.

JEROME K. JEROME

No matter how much cats fight, there always seem to be plenty of kittens.

ABRAHAM LINCOLN

It is a very inconvenient habit of kittens (Alice had once made the remark) that whatever you say to them, they always purr.

> LEWIS CARROLL, *Through the Looking-Glass, and What Alice Found There*

An ordinary kitten will ask more questions than any five-year-old.

> CARL VAN VECHTEN

It is impossible to keep a straight face in the presence of one or more kittens.

> CYNTHIA E. VARNADO

The playful kitten, with its pretty little tigerish gambols, is infinitely more amusing than half the people one is obliged to live with in the world.

LADY SYDNEY MORGAN

Confront a child, a puppy, and a kitten with a sudden danger; the child will turn instinctively for assistance, the puppy will grovel in abject submission, the kitten will brace its tiny body for a frantic resistance.

SAKI

One small cat changes coming home to an empty house to coming home.

PAM BROWN

Do you see that kitten chasing so prettily her own tail? If you could look with her eyes, you might see her surrounded with hundreds of figures performing complex dramas, with tragic and comic issues, long conversations, many characters, many ups and downs of fate.

Ralph Waldo Emerson

Are we really sure the purring is coming from the kitty and not from our very own hearts?

Terri Guillemets

# COMICAL
# CATS

Cat's motto: No matter what you've done wrong, always try to make it look like the dog did it.

AUTHOR UNKNOWN

Those who'll play with cats must expect to be scratched.

MIGUEL DE CERVANTES

There is, incidentally, no way of talking about cats that enables one to come off as a sane person.

DAN GREENBERG

CAT (n): 1. Furry keyboard cover
2. Alarm clock

AUTHOR UNKNOWN

When moving to a new home, always put the cat through the window instead of the door, so that it will not leave.

AMERICAN PROVERB

The household cat is really a tiger that has underwent three counselling programs.

VALERIU BUTULESCU

I think all cats are wild. They only act tame if there's a saucer of milk in it for them.

DOUGLAS ADAMS

Cats regard people as warm-blooded furniture.

JACQUELYN MITCHARD

No amount of time can erase the memory of a good cat, and no amount of masking tape can ever totally remove his fur from your couch.

LEO DWORKEN

Your cat will never threaten your popularity by barking at three in the morning. He won't attack the mailman or eat the drapes, although he may climb the drapes to see how the room looks from the ceiling.

HELEN POWERS

To err is human. To purr feline.

ROBERT BRYNE

Any household with at least one feline member has no need for an alarm clock.

LOUISE A. BELCHER

Never ask a hungry cat whether he loves you for yourself alone.

DR. LOUIS J. CAMUTI

Your cat may never have to hunt farther than the kitchen counter for its supper nor face a predator fiercer than the vacuum cleaner.

BARBARA L. DIAMOND

A cat has a reputation to protect. If it had a halo, it would be worn cocked to one side.

WILL DURANT

To bathe a cat takes brute force, perseverance, courage of conviction—and a cat. The last ingredient is usually hardest to come by.

STEPHEN BAKER

I had been told that the training procedure with cats was difficult. It's not. Mine had me trained in two days.

BILL DANA

Cats are the ultimate narcissists. You can tell this because of all the time they spend on personal grooming. Dogs aren't like this. A dog's idea of personal grooming is to roll in a dead fish.

JAMES GORMAN

Even if you have just destroyed a Ming vase, purr. Usually all will be forgiven.

LENNY RUBENSTEIN

One is never sure, watching two cats washing each other, whether it's affection, the taste or a trial run for the jugular.

HELEN THOMSON

A cat's worst enemy is a closed door.

AUTHOR UNKNOWN

One cat just leads to another.

ERNEST HEMINGWAY

He swings from the chandelier, he paws my peanut butter, and he knocks over my drink in the most unfortunate places in the house—but I still love him like crazy. It's like a hairball in my heart.

AUDRA FOVEO-ALBA

Never try to out stubborn a cat.

ROBERT A. HEINLEIN

I rarely meddled in the cat's personal affairs and she rarely meddled in mine. Neither of us was foolish enough to attribute human emotions to our pets.

KINKY FRIEDMAN

The way to keep a cat is to try to chase it away.

E.W. HOWE

A black cat crossing your path signifies that the animal is going somewhere.

GROUCHO MARX

I'm sorry that I'm not updating my Facebook status, my cat ate my mouse.

ANONYMOUS

If you hold a cat by the tail, you learn things you cannot learn any other way.

MARK TWAIN

If it's raining at the back door, every cat is convinced there's a good chance it won't be raining at the front door.

WILLIAM TOMS

I read that when cats are cuddling and kneading you, and you think it's cute, they're really just checking your vitals for weak spots.

KANDYSE MCCLURE

If the grass looked greener on my side of the fence, it was because my cats kept pee-ing near it.

SHANNON L. ADLER

The cat could very well be man's best friend but would never stoop to admitting it.

DOUG LARSON

There is no snooze button on a cat who wants breakfast.

AUTHOR UNKNOWN

People that hate cats will come back as mice in their next life.

FAITH RESNICK

Behind every slightly confused looking dog there's a cat laughing maniacally.

AUTHOR UNKNOWN

Any cat who misses a mouse pretends it was aiming for the dead leaf.

CHARLOTTE GRAY

The problem with cats is they get the exact same look whether they see a moth or an ax-murderer.

PAULA POUNDSTONE

Most beds sleep up to six cats. Ten cats without the owner.

STEPHEN BAKER

A dog is a dog, a bird is a bird, and a cat is a person.

MUGSY PEABODY

When you come upon your cat, deep in meditation, staring thoughtfully at something that you can't see, just remember that your cat is, in fact, running the universe.

BONNI ELIZABETH HALL

It's really the cat's house—we just pay the mortgage.

AUTHOR UNKNOWN

Cats are smarter than dogs. You can't get eight cats to pull a sled through snow.

JEFF VALDEZ

# FOR THE
# LOVE
# OF CATS

A cat does not want all the world to love her—only those she has chosen to love.

HELEN THOMSON

Only cat lovers know the luxury of fur-coated, musical hot water bottles that never go cold.

SUSANNE MILLEN

I love cats because I enjoy my home; and, little by little, they become its visible soul.

JEAN COCTEAU

The difference between friends and pets
is that friends we allow into our company,
pets we allow into our solitude.

ROBERT BRAULT

There is something about the presence of
a cat... that seems to take the bite out of
being alone.

LOUIS J. CAMUTI

The human race can be roughly divided
into two categories: ailurophiles and
ailurophobes—cat lovers and the
underprivileged.

DAVID TAYLOR

When a cat flatters...he is not insincere: you may safely take it for real kindness.

WALTER SAVAGE LANDOR

It is a well-known fact that the survival rate after heart attacks is significantly higher among pet owners than non-owners, and that human blood pressure falls in the presence of companion animals—especially cats.

DR. MAYA PATEL

Cats are a tonic, they are a laugh, they are a cuddle, they are at least pretty just about all of the time and beautiful some of the time.

ROGER CARAS

To some blind souls all cats are much alike. To a cat lover every cat from the beginning of time has been utterly and amazingly unique.

JENNY DE VRIES

Purring would seem to be, in her case, an automatic safety-valve device for dealing with happiness overflow.

MONICA EDWARDS

Cats look beyond appearances—beyond species entirely, it seems—to peer into the heart.

BARBARA L. DIAMOND

If you would know a man, observe how he treats a cat.

ROBERT A. HEINLEIN

It is difficult to obtain the friendship of a cat. It is a philosophic animal—one that does not place its affections thoughtlessly.

THEOPHILE GAUTIER

Cats are distant, discreet, impeccably clean and able to stay silent. What more could be needed to be good company?

MARIE LECINSKA

A cat improves the garden wall in sunshine, and the hearth in foul weather.

JUDITH MERKLE RILEY

Every life should have nine cats.

AUTHOR UNKNOWN

I regard cats as one of the great joys in the world. I see them as a gift of highest order.

TRISHA McCAGH

If purring could be encapsulated, it'd be the most powerful anti-depressant on the pharmaceutical market.

ALEXIS F. HOPE

No man or woman can be called friendless
who has the companionship of a cat.

JAMES LAUTNER

There is nothing sweeter than his peace
when at rest, for there is nothing brisker
than his life when in motion.

CHRISTOPHER SMART

You will always be lucky if you know how
to make friends with strange cats.

COLONIAL AMERICAN PROVERB

A cat can be trusted to purr when she is pleased, which is more than can be said for human beings.

WILLIAM RALPH INGE

There are two means of refuge from the miseries of life: music and cats.

ALBERT SCHWEITZER

It is impossible for a lover of cats to banish these alert, gentle, and discriminating little friends, who give us just enough of their regard and complaisance to make us hunger for more.

AGNES REPPLIER

What greater gift than the love of a cat?

CHARLES DICKENS

If we treated everyone with the same affection we bestow upon our favorite cat, they, too, would purr.

MARTIN BUXBAUM

I have felt cats rubbing their faces against mine and touching cheek with claws carefully sheathed. These things, to me, are expressions of love.

JAMES HERRIOT

How do you summon up courage to dismiss a cat who is paying you a compliment of sitting on your lap?

DEREK TANGYE

Never underestimate the power of a purr.

ANONYMOUS

Very few human beings are privileged to know the cat.

MICHAEL JOSEPH